Living Sexy

To Lisa,
Keep on Living
Sexy

ANNETTE SANNIOTA

Annette

Printed in the United States of America

First Printing, 2019

ISBN: 978-1-54398-917-5

BookBaby Publishing
7905 N. Crescent Blvd.
Pennsauken, NJ 08110

www.BookBaby.com

Dedicated to my family for always loving
me throughout our circle of life.

I thank God for every single blessing
even when it did not appear as one.

TABLE OF CONTENTS

1   Preface

3   Living Sexy

7   Confidence VS Arrogance

9   The Positive Aspect of Difficult Times

11 Being Satisfied With What You Have

13 Positive VS Negative

15 Accept Who You Are

19 Beige VS Champagne, Oyster and Pearl

21 You Are What You Eat – Drink Water – Don't Smoke!

25 Age Sexy

27 Celebrate Your Birthday Month

29 Be Friendly With Your Ex(es)

31 You Can't Control the Actions of Others

33 My Miracle, Thank God

39 First Love

43 God as Navigator

47 Self-Respect

49 You Might Have a Bad Hair Day

51 What is My Assignment?

55 The Balance

57 Cheers To Living Your Best Life!

Preface

·····························

This handbook is written with the intent to share my personal feelings and opinions. While I believe this to be a positive, happy, useful tool, there may be some who read it who question the validity and that is normal and expected. The truth is that life does not present us with only positive situations, decisions, people or expectations, and certainly *does* present us with heartache, regret and loneliness at times. The whole purpose of, and what I believe to be the secret to, *Living Sexy* is the ability to see your situation as a positive blessing that is happening in your life at this time for a specific reason. Sometimes we cannot see the reason. My go to response for everything is finding the blessing that may be really hidden in a terrible scenario. My personal belief is that everything has a blessing. Our attitude creates our aura and how others perceive us. You will learn a lot about me and while I am always looking for a positive outcome, you will notice that some things that I have experienced did not initially appear as positive. This handbook is for you to perhaps try viewing your circumstances through a different lens and thus profoundly change your expectations about the good, the bad, the ugly and the beautiful with the hope that you learn to love yourself and look for the best in others. I hope you enjoy it and may it shine a light in your life!

Living Sexy

....

My name is Annette, my nickname is Net Net which was originally bestowed upon me from my nephew when he was a toddler over 22 years ago and has since spread through my adult social circles. I am 53 years old. I am single. I am divorced…twice. I am a daughter, a mother, a sister, an aunt, a cousin, a friend, an encourager and an independent lady. I have an amazing career. I love where I live. I am happy. I am fabulous. I am sexy.

The purpose of this writing is to share with anyone at any age the secrets of living sexy. It doesn't begin or end in your twenties, thirties, forties or fifties or ever! In fact, sexiness is perennial, it is a mindset, we can be sexy our entire lives! It is a belief…an attitude…in fact, being happy is all about your attitude. You make a choice to be happy or to be anything else! This writing will give you ideas on how to create your own "sexy" and live it – everyday! Life is beautiful if you see it that way. You are sexy if you see it that way.

No need for cosmetic surgery, no need to change the person you are. In fact, true beauty really does come from within. Have you ever seen an outwardly gorgeous man or woman and moments later you were disappointed from how not beautiful this outwardly beautiful person was? Conversely, have you ever seen a not-so-attractive person and when he/she begins to speak, you see an aura of beauty and love and feel the true person inside the package? And you are compelled to like this person, to love this person. This is the focus of what you are reading.

While this guide to living sexy is not intended for women only, there are some poignant topics that may be directed towards women but remember, men can grasp an understanding here too for the women they love. The first item is the lie that has been passed down to all women for generations stating that menopause is the end of womanhood, the beginning of unwanted hair in unwanted places, the beginning of the "END"! WOW, it is just the opposite! It is the beginning of the best time of your life IF YOU CHOOSE TO VIEW IT AS SUCH. You reach the point where you know what you want, you know what you like, you do what you want and THAT makes you sexy! The unwanted hair thing, well, if it happens, get it removed! What is the problem? It is scary to hear the horror stories of the "curse" when you get your period in your teens and then the horror stories of "the end" when you get in your fifties. Really sounds like a methodology of trying to keep people oppressed and feeling inadequate and never good enough. I am here to tell you that none of that is true. You are beautiful, strong and fabulous and yes, sexy.

But…you need to believe it. When a woman believes it, her partner believes it too.

Confidence VS Arrogance

....

Confidence may be the most important accessory you wear. Confidence is very sexy. But be careful, arrogance is ugly. In fact, being happy with yourself and wearing that happiness when you enter a room, when you are conducting a meeting, when you meet new people – creates the sexy person that is inside you. For clarity, I have taken the definitions of both words from Dictionary.com.

> Confidence- 1. Full trust; belief in the powers, trustworthiness, or reliability of a person or thing, 2. Belief in oneself and one's powers or abilities; self-confidence; self-reliance; assurance

> Arrogance- 1. Offensive display of superiority or self-importance; overbearing pride.

You probably knew the difference between the words but sometimes seeing it on paper really makes a difference.

We have all known those people who are arrogant and lack humility and yes, these attributes are indeed ugly.

I want you to think about confidence as an accessory. Think about wearing it when you are getting dressed for work or an outing. Think about how you feel in your confidence. Know you are beautiful. Be thankful and filled with gratitude for another day of life. Be the reason someone smiles. Be in control of your "fabulosity"**. You will come to understand how your fabulosity becomes an integral part of your sexy as you continue to read. People will love being around you because of how you make people feel.

Wear your confidence daily, live sexy every day.

** *I enjoy creating new words and I actually utilize these words in my daily life. It's ok. I define Fabulosity as encompassing the confidence accessory and showing it always.*

The Positive Aspect of Difficult Times

....

No matter how fabulous you are and try to be, you will inevitably encounter difficult times in your life. We all do. We have to. If you think about being on vacation when every day is fun, you really look forward to the time when you go home to your home and enjoy your life. Don't worry, I am not knocking vacations! They are a necessary aspect of living and necessary for people to decompress, regroup, focus and be prepared for your real life.

Now take that concept and apply it to your everyday life. You have heard that you need the rain to appreciate the sun. Rain isn't actually a negative thing because it provides growth and nutrients to our earth, plants, landscaping and flowers. The result of rain gives beautiful life. It just seems that while it is raining and you may have wanted to spend the day outdoors it interferes with your plans. This is true of difficult times.

Going through a trying time where you might think you cannot bear or go on actually gives you the tools to live a life of gratitude. Close your eyes and remember a time where your life was going in a seemingly wrong direction; perhaps during that time you couldn't see that it was wrong but the results that followed were magical. Sometimes it can take years of a difficult time. This happened to me. This was a time I was not living sexy.

If I did not live through this portion of my life, I would not be who I am today. I learned a lifesaving lesson in relationships. The length of the difficult times was approximately 5 years in total. I didn't think I would survive. Not only did I survive, I thrived.

Do I wish this difficult time in my history never happened? To be truthful, I believe it was necessary to live through so that I could learn the lesson I needed to learn at that time. I therefore cannot say that I wish it never happened. In fact, in a way, I am forever thankful that I did live through it, I endured, I survived the pain and recognized the importance of my family. I am filled with gratitude and make the choice to look at the positive results VS the negative situation.

Make the choice to always see the positive in any situation…now THAT is living sexy.

Being Satisfied With What You Have

....

Part of true inner beauty that shines through your eyes regardless of how physically beautiful you are is the gratitude you feel with everything you have. When you believe you are happy, you start to manifest this joy through your actions. Realizing that everyone has problems, that no one has a perfect life, that physical pain can afflict us from time to time is important. It is unrealistic to think that you are alone in your pain or suffering. How we choose to deal with the pain is the true answer. Loving your life and knowing you are filled with gratitude for everything you have is a magnetic power that exudes from your inner self to your outer self and shines. People will be drawn to you and will like you. They will. I believe in the power of gratitude. When bad things happen, people tend to wallow in their problems. Of course, some problems are very grave and require an appropriate time for grieving but this is not what this writing is about. Living Sexy is about focusing on your day to day life and living it in such a way that makes you look fabulous because you feel fabulous and it is leaping off your person! Remember the word "fabulosity"? This is what Living Sexy is illustrating. Find your fabulosity by being filled with gratitude and love and your fabulosity will emerge. It happens every time.

Positive VS Negative

....

Every day we make choices. In fact, every minute of every day we are in control of how we choose to feel. If you take control over the exterior forces that try and rule or ruin your day, you begin to see that you really can change how your body reacts. We do not have any control over what people say or how they treat us, but we always have control over how we react. This is the choice for being positive always.

Of course, we are not robots. We have feelings and we do get upset, it happens all the time. What you have to focus on, though, is to recognize when this occurs. Recognize that just because this person did or said something that offends you; choose to believe perhaps this person is having a bad day. Maybe this person is on medication or maybe they are having difficult times at home with a spouse or children. Maybe this person is just sad and lashing out at the world.

You and I can make the choice to respond positively to these people and who knows maybe make a difference in their day.

Most of my professional life I was a licensed condo community association manager. Interestingly, I happened into this position, it wasn't my course of study. What is more interesting is that in this business you are dealing with homeowners who live in the communities that you manage. Of course there are issues that arise that may involve neighbor to neighbor and I always made a valiant effort to keep the peace. Living in a community where there is stress or strife cannot add to your quality of life so as Manager I would listen and then resolve. And I kept private comments private. In a way, I helped to foster the positive aspect of the community while maintaining its rules and lifestyle.

In my late twenties, while managing a luxury hi rise condo, I learned a valuable lesson that there may be people who might not like me. Back then I could not accept this as a truth because I always tried to be kind to people. Today, however, I understand and accept this and actually laugh about some experiences typically over Happy Hour with my friends. I choose to turn this seemingly bad thing into a positive. I utilize the mindset to choose to find the positive because I make efforts to empathize with people who may be having a bad day or a bad situation is upon them. Laughing is really important. Laughing at oneself is key; trying not to take yourself too seriously and looking at the positive are ways to live sexy.

Accept Who You Are

....

We all have friends who are single and those who are married. There is no right answer to be one or the other. Ironically, though, I tend to note that the married people sometimes secretly envy the singles and the singles sometimes secretly envy the married ones. I believe this observation in and of itself holds a magical key to Living Sexy. Here is the key: being content with what you have or where you are in life.

Living Sexy isn't about looking to become single or married but about accepting and embracing with positive joy the exact place you are in your journey. Circumstances change and instead of finding the negative in those changes, look for the positive. If you find the love of your life and you stay together for a lifetime that is a truly beautiful love story. Celebrate this if it is you, and if it isn't you but you know someone who is in a relationship like this, celebrate for them! What a glorious scenario!

I have been single for most of my adult life even with the two marriages. I truly believe I learned invaluable life lessons from both and while the second ended very financially and emotionally draining for me at that moment in time, I am thankful and so blessed for being able to live through that and come out of it still a positive being. With that said, I am happily single. You don't hear that often but it really is true for me. People ask me all the time if I date and wow they can't believe someone hasn't just swooped me up. This is so interesting and really flattering. The truth is, until I meet someone who is right for me, who is my equal in all aspects, I choose to remain happily single.

Self-respect now becomes the primary discussion. Love yourself. Recognize that you are wonderful and filled with fabulosity. You don't need to be defined by another person. You are enough. You have the ability to live independently and positively. If you find someone who adds joy and peace to your life and contributes to your whole amazing self, then give yourself permission to go that route.

I hope we all can achieve becoming the love of our own lives. Another secret to *Living Sexy* is believing that beauty from within becomes the focal point of me, of you, of all of us. You know that beautiful person when you are at work or just walking down the street. You feel that fabulosity. Once you really love yourself, "que será, será". You will show this on your face and through your eyes and deep within your soul. This isn't a lie. In fact, it's pretty sexy.

Beige VS Champagne, Oyster and Pearl

....

I purchased a new preowned car. It was elegant, beautiful and really sexy. The color was beige as listed on the manufacturer's specification sheet. When I showed my best friend my new car, she commented how beautiful the color was and wanted to know the name. I told her the manufacturer's sheet called it beige but that I didn't think it looked beige to me – that it looked more like champagne. She suggested perhaps oyster or pearl but definitely not beige for "Net Net". When you read those descriptive colors, could you immediately see the nuances in each of those colors? Did you see the champagne color as sleek and the oyster or pearl with a subtle glow and shine? You did.

Is this a big deal? Of course not, but when you are *Living Sexy* each part of your life plays a significant role in how you carry yourself and how you feel inside. We must not underestimate the power of the little things, as so many of us do, sometimes without even realizing it. Each time you practice living sexy you become better at it, and you start to see opportunities to incorporate this philosophy everywhere.

What about the colors silver and gray? Silver sounds sexy and gray sounds drab. There may be almost exact colors in the different hues of each of these individual colors but choosing to use silver in place of gray seems to change your response to it.

Be good to yourself, see the beauty in everything. Nothing is drab when you see beauty.

Try describing the vitality you see in all things on a regular basis. Appreciate the beauty that is always available. A blue sky can be described as something so much more. Seeing the blue sky instead as a sky with depth of blues, greens and every subliminal hue in between whispers more poetically to our souls. This description allows you to feel the magnitude of the sky's beauty. Having the ability to feel and see colors creates art in your life.

Seeing the beauty in all living things is really sexy.

You Are What You Eat – Drink Water – Don't Smoke!

....

Treat your body and your mind with respect and love. Eat foods that make you feel GOOD after you've eaten. Treat yourself to a delectable dessert now and then, don't ever feel like you are denying yourself pleasure. We do get pleasure from flavors and that is good for our souls. I try not to get pigeon-holed with a boring menu and instead look in my refrigerator, assess what flavors are there and then plan a dinner recipe that is usually fabulous. This makes your meal planning exciting and creative and well, yes, sexy. Picking easy, processed foods may seem to save time but you are depriving yourself of what your body really needs. A balanced diet is necessary to have a healthy body and mind.

You are also a reflection of the people with whom you choose to spend time. Think about that one for a minute. If you are enjoying an evening with friends or family who are uplifting and happy and who look for the best in life, you will experience joy. If you instead choose to spend time with people who are looking at the negative, or trying to bring you down either by words or substances, you will experience restlessness and a constant urge to find something that will make you feel better. Good friends, supportive family and a healthy diet will make you better. This will happen every time, always.

Living Sexy always refers to attitude, life choices and the joy we feel when we truly love ourselves. If you live alone, don't deprive yourself of a healthy, delicious dinner because you are only one person and there is no one else to cook for. Aren't you worth it?

Yes, you're worth it. And THAT is sexy.

One of the easiest things we can do every day is drink water! Hydrating your body is so essential to keeping your insides as well as your outsides in a prime healthy state. If you drink sodas on a regular basis, try to gradually reduce that consumption a little at a time. Make small realistic goals so that you don't feel so bad if you go backwards here and there. I think we tend to be so unforgiving of ourselves if we fall short of what our own expectations are. That is why dieting really doesn't work in the long run. Monitoring what we eat which means monitoring our diet is what keeps us healthy and successful. If you really believe that everything you put in your body has some type of effect, whether positive or negative you can control your diet. Water is a magical substance that keeps your skin beautiful and keeps your body hydrated and healthy.

Smoking does the exact opposite of that! Yes, smoking is both a real and serious addiction and if you currently smoke, do whatever you can to stop. Your life is dependent on that. With every glass of water you are contributing to a healthier lifestyle both physically and mentally – with every cigarette you are contributing to an unhealthy lifestyle that never ends positively. Cigarettes rob your skin of oxygen and elasticity, contribute to deep chest coughing, cause all types of diseases which we can't even begin to name and are a HUGE budgetary item. Cigarettes make you smell bad, from the inside out. Of course the best choice is to never start. But if you are a smoker, look for the resources that are available to help you quit so that you can become your best self. Be with people that will support you for trying to quit and try to avoid those who make you want to smoke more.

Clean lungs are sexy!

Age Sexy

....

Yes, we all age. Hopefully, we all age, the alternative is not so positive. So knowing aging is a natural process and things in our body and on our body are going to get older, it is extremely important to accept the natural process and not fight it. With that said, if you are taking care of your mind and your body and are eating right and sleeping enough, your body will age gently and gradually. I just saw photos of once beautiful movie stars who had taken the route of cosmetic surgery. What is ironic about this is the ones who have gone the cosmetic surgery route were truly physically beautiful at least by the world's standards. That is sad to me. It is sad because these beautiful people really felt their outward beauty as only skin deep and attempted to preserve their youth. We shouldn't fall into this pit of deception because you can't preserve your youth – you can't look young forever. But you really can BE beautiful forever with the right attitude.

I have never been an athletic person. I started exercising in my late 40's. I am not very coordinated and well, am pretty dizzy when I walk! Instead of focusing on what I can't do, I focus on everything I CAN do! I can walk! There are people who cannot walk and may be limited to a wheelchair but everyone has the opportunity to take in God's beauty. Why not go outside, breathe the fresh air and listen to your music or whatever it is that brings you joy. Sometimes I like to meditate during my time alone and respect the quiet moments. It is a truly beautiful gift to be thankful and grateful for every little thing you have. Always remember that every day alive is a gift.

Today and every day thereafter, think of something that you can do right now and do it. When you pick a meal, try and pick foods that will enhance your body and mind and keep them both happy and healthy. Live each day to the fullest and have a thankful heart for all that you have. That joy will show on your face and in your words and people will be drawn to you. You will inadvertently share happiness just by being a happy you.

Sexy is timeless and has no age.

Celebrate Your Birthday Month

....

Why not celebrate your birthday month? Isn't it a blessing to become older each year? Each year you live you hopefully learn more, help others more, live better and love better. Tell everyone it's your birthday! Happy people are infectious to others – in a good way! Happy people emit a positive vibe and every person in that presence feels good. It is magical. It is not drug induced! It is just your mind being positive and always looking at the good. I promise when you tell people it's your birthday month, they will smile and will wish you happy thoughts.

Getting older is fabulous. You know so much more about yourself and others. You can choose to be happy and tolerant of others which really makes you a magnet for others. You could choose to be sad, wishing you were young again, judgmental on others and miserable too – I promise if you choose this route you will not be a magnet for others!

Be happy, accept your birthday and celebrate the fabulosity that is YOU!

During my history and my evolution of becoming the me I am today, I once practiced a religion that did not condone the celebration of holidays including birthdays. The premise of this belief was that if you celebrated birthdays or holidays, you were taking away from your worship of God and instead redirecting your attention to self or the other holidays. Instead, I choose to view the birthday as a celebration that you were created, conceived and became a beautiful living being which in my opinion is the closest thing to praising God for a truly magical gift. I try and always look at the positive side of any situation. I believe in being a positive force in this world. I thank God for my birthday and for each day and each year of life my family and loved ones are here to share with me. I thank God for their birthdays. Smile, there is so much to be thankful for.

Be Friendly With Your Ex(es)

·······················

While this friendly advice may not always be possible or appropriate, it does heal one's soul to be able to be cordial when you see an ex out and about. This rule of thumb I believe also applies to seeing friends that are no longer friends. If you live your life believing that life is too short to have negative thoughts and feelings and realize that holding grudges ONLY affects you, then you are Living Sexy. I could truthfully write an entire biographical novel depicting events that happened to me by others who really hurt me deeply. I definitely don't want to mislead you by thinking my relationships have all been a bed of roses! However, I do want to stress the importance of forgiveness and moving on. There is such peace and happiness when you take control of a situation and manage it properly and move on. You won't want to hang out with that person and you should not. But you need to feel confident in the knowledge that forgiving that person really gives you the ability to not hold grudges and not wish revenge and basically just lets you live your life. Always live your life knowing that it is fleeting and each moment is a true gift. Be compassionate with others always but don't be used. Love, forgive and know when to walk away with grace and dignity.

That's Living S[ex]y.

You Can't Control the Actions of Others

....

This thought might just be the secret to life. How many times a day or week have you experienced someone treating you unfairly or badly? Your first feeling or response is probably anger or the thought of revenge or something in the negative realm. Don't worry, this is normal, these feelings are reasons we are imperfect humans. My suggestion is to acknowledge that your feelings are valid because feelings are emotional not rational. Here is where I would urge a change in attitude. Recognize that you were hurt, recognize that your feelings are normal and valid, but then, make the CHOICE to REACT in a positive way or thought process. When we realize that we cannot control what other people say or do, we find ourselves in an unusual position of control. Internal control of your reactions is extremely empowering. This idea goes together with thinking positively and having a positive attitude every day. It is not easy. In fact, you should never take it for granted when you are "taking the high road," that doing so was a simple decision. Looking for the positive in every situation, giving others the benefit of the doubt and believing that they may be going through something we cannot even imagine, are ways we take control of our lives and our feelings and emotions. Be proud of yourself for trying to do the right thing even when no one is watching. Doing the right thing without acknowledgment by others is very gratifying and defines your integrity. Make a goal each day to take control of your reactions and watch how the universe shifts in your favor. It happens every time, always.

Forgive yourself. By remembering we are imperfect and we may have done someone wrong at some point in our history, it is good to ask for forgiveness from yourself. I know in past years during the low point of my history, I was so low that I must have exhibited inappropriate behavior or negatively affected certain people. Forgive yourself. Learn from your mistakes. Care for others.

Having empathy is sexy.

My Miracle, Thank God

....

I do not intend for this writing to be religious or trying to influence others to believe what I believe. I do however feel it is important to know who I am as a person and why perhaps I live the way I live and believe what I believe.

It is no secret to my family and friends that I love God. God and I have had a relationship my whole life but as most, that relationship has gone through many changes and evolutions through the years. I was raised Catholic with my very close Italian family. In fact my parents' story is another book to be written; I believe my son will tackle that one! But to summarize, my parents were both born in Naples, Italy and my father's family migrated to the United States when he was a little boy of 9. His family moved to a farm in North Carolina and my father's life changed from living in a bustling metropolis of Naples to living a farmer's life. Fast forward to his high school graduation and enlistment in the

US Navy, he returned to Naples and met my mother. This is such a miraculous story in and of itself, but for the purposes of this writing, my parents met on July 1, my father proposed on July 3, and they were married in an Italian, Catholic wedding with the approval of the Catholic Church in America and my father's naval officer in command.

I know you have so many questions, but the best part of this story is that through a lifetime of changes, challenges, growth, confusion, language barriers, business partners and parental partners, my parents just celebrated their 55th wedding anniversary.

I have been divorced twice.

Getting divorced was never in my life plans! Being raised a particular way does not guarantee our expectations. I was always a type A personality, straight A's and B's, National Honor Society, neat freak, need I say more? So my plans to marry Mr. Right and have 2.5 children and stay married forever, however, did not fit in with God's perfect plan for me.

Let's go back a few years to when I was twelve. I was sailing in our lake behind our house in Florida, with full parental supervision and the boat started to take on water. I was sailing with my friend (neighbor) who was really scared so I jumped into the water, grabbed the boat by the bow and started pulling it to shore. My dad was monitoring and helped immediately, and he knew I was very well equipped to handle this scenario. Once ashore, I realized I had pulled a muscle and was so sore the next day that my mom had to take me to the doctor. The doctor confirmed it was just a muscle pull but upon examination, he noticed my spine had a curve instead of it being straight. He recommended I go to a specialist and the day my mom and I learned I was diagnosed with Scoliosis; we thought it was the end! The prognosis was for me to wear a back brace that fully encompassed my entire upper body to my hips that attached in the back with really large metal brackets in the back and a super large metal bracket in the front that also encircled my neck. Needless to say, this was NOT sexy! But I wanted to share this event for two reasons: the first is that without that odd sailing episode, I would not have found out about this condition which could have, and probably would have, resulted in an extensive spinal surgery at the best scenario and/or the possibility of having a heart condition by 40 and the inability to have children (by the way, this was what the specialist told my mother and me at the time to ensure we decided to wear the brace!); the second is that the brace became a true blessing to me and my ability to feel empathy for others and try to always look for the best. I wore this brace full time for 8th and 9th grades which was very challenging. At the ages of 12 and 13 an adolescent usually is trying to figure out so many things so dealing with this very noticeable contraption was not a simple obstacle to overcome. This is where God intervened again.

I was going to Catholic school in 9th grade and my Theology teacher Sister Jane was telling a story about St. Teresa, the little flower. It certainly must have made a big impact to me in class because I went home and said the prayer. The prayer to St. Teresa is praying for her intervention with God through Jesus to ask for a blessing. You say the prayer for ten days and when the prayer is answered, St. Teresa sends you flowers from heaven. Sounds so nice and to a 14 year old trapped in this brace, it was worth a try!

Now I need to tell you another part of this miracle story that perhaps seemed unrelated but was part of the overall plan. For whatever reason, my mother and my sister had purchased some flower seeds some weeks prior. My sister was so discouraged because these seeds never sprouted, never flowered and her plan to grow flowers was thwarted.

About 3 weeks or so after I had completed my ten days of praying for St. Teresa's intervention, the miracle happened. You need to know that prior to this date at the age of 14, I had never been given any flowers. Also, you must know, I NEVER spoke of this prayer to my parents or sister as I was sort of testing Sister Jane's teaching. One morning for no apparent reason, my mom was sitting on the patio having her morning coffee and she was compelled to look into the area where my sister had planted the flower seeds that never bloomed. My mother got up and walked over and saw one flower in full bloom. Just one. She asked my sister to cut the flower from the soil and brought it inside. My mother cannot explain why she did this but she called me and told me she wanted to give me the flower. At the time, I had momentarily forgotten about the prayer and suddenly it hit me and I got chills and started crying and told my mother I had prayed to St. Teresa. Now my mother was crying! To confirm this one flower was the answer to my prayer, the stem of the flower was crooked, sort of like an "S" which was the curvature of my spine. At my next doctor appointment, the doctor confirmed my spine had straightened 5 degrees which gave him the ability to tell me that I did not have to wear the brace to school any longer. This was truly a miracle. I was able to start 10th grade in a new high school without the brace. I wore the brace at night and slept with it until I was 19.

I am so thankful to God for the trials, the awakenings I have had in my life. I am thankful that his plan was for me to have one son who is truly an amazing person with a beautiful soul. Life is about being peaceful even when there is turmoil, trying to always find the bright light about every situation.

First Love

....

I think we all have had one. It was perfect, pure, real, loving, special, amazing and breath-taking and what we defined at the time as true. Maybe it was? Maybe it happened for a reason. Maybe we need to learn at a younger age what those intense feelings are because it is only at that point in our existence that we have nothing to compare it to. The fact that it was the first and that it was so intense and that it was so real is why that first love will always be perfect.

I did not intend to write about my first love but because that perfect memory still haunts me at times, I felt it was interesting enough to share and you will probably identify with it as well. I also want to point out that at times in our personal history we believe we are in the right scenario and try and force the outcome of our expectations. But as we just discussed previously, sometimes our expectations are not the reality we live. So with that in mind, remember that identifying your sexy through another person is a fleeting concept.

So...

Remember the first moment when you see that person? For me the first time I had an encounter with him was at the beach in the summer of 1983 after my high school graduation. He walked up with a group of friends whom I knew but I had never been introduced to him. A day or two later I was home with my family and the phone rang – remember the wall phones with the rotary dial – yes this was 1983! When I answered the phone and this sweet unknown voice asked to speak with me and identified himself, I cannot describe the absolute physical reaction I had with full on butterflies and the feeling of maybe passing out? He asked if I would like to go to dinner and a movie with him later that week. I of course said yes and when I hung up the phone, I was a giddy, happy, silly 17 year old teenager describing him to my family and counting the hours until our first date.

The first date was awesome and really speaks to the kind of person he was. He knocked on my door, I think I must have introduced him to my mom and we then went to the car. He was driving one of the family's cars which he sheepishly warned me that his brother had something not so pleasant smelling in the car earlier that day and he had tried to make it smell better but I think it smelled of lemon pledge or something really strong. Not only was it a sweet gesture that he was trying to make this night so special, it was so completely endearing. He opened my door and we were off to a beautiful oceanfront restaurant for dinner.

I had been so concerned about what to talk about during dinner and when I was preparing for the date and talking to my mom she very confidently told me I would have no problem creating conversation (she was right, she is always right). She also advised me to not eat broccoli because I wouldn't want to have that stuck in my teeth!

Dinner was magical. He was magical. Everything was perfect. He opened the car door for me to sit and when He got into the car, he reached behind the seat and handed me a beautiful bouquet of flowers. I was so surprised and I thanked him and asked why he had decided to give them to me then. He very comfortably replied, "I didn't know if I was going to like you" – this really resonated with me because it was then that I knew giving flowers was not just a guy move he would do. I knew then that he was real and a genuine gentleman.

We were together for two and one half years, dating long distance during the college years and the break up occurred because of a difference in philosophy. We both cried and it ended. I was married 8 months later to a different man. Five years later, I gave birth to my one and only son. It truly becomes clear that God's plan prevailed and He knew the only way my son Austin would be who he is today is with the combination of his father and myself. There can be no other explanation. Austin is an incredible young man.

Life happens. We grow, we learn, we live, we laugh, we cry, we wish we made different decisions but learn quickly that we cannot turn back time.

Accepting life's mysteries and gifts with a smile is sexy!

God as Navigator

....

Can you imagine driving on an interstate highway in the middle of rush hour, losing control and doing 3- 360's from the left lane across three lanes to end up in the emergency lane on the far right side of the road facing oncoming traffic six inches away from the guard rail without so much as a scratch on the car or passengers?

This is a miraculous story. My sister was driving, I was in the passenger seat, my 5 year old son was in the back seat in a car seat and my sister's 2 year old baby was in the baby seat in the back seat next to him. This event was a typical drive to deliver my nephew to his father for visitation and the scenario was always scary. My nephew even at that young age hated going there and would come back feeling anxious and crying and sad. Needless to say, this routine was taxing and beyond stressful for my sister and my family. Watching a baby who otherwise was a smiley, bubbly personality fall into unspoken stress and turmoil was almost unbearable.

It was during a return visit from picking up my nephew that my sister and I were having a heart to heart conversation about these events and scenarios and the inability to make any changes and we were commiserating over the inability to control anything. My sister had the car in cruise control, driving the regular speed and there was just a light rain. Suddenly we felt the car lift. It is difficult to explain what we felt but my sister remained in control the entire time. When she tells this story, you feel like you were there. She knew the car was lifting from the road and she maintained the steering wheel, somehow disengaged the cruise control and we spun around and around and around. The fact that we were placed 6 inches from the guard rail, with never any impact is miraculous enough. But what I still cannot understand is HOW no other cars hit us. The entire event must have taken 20 – 30 seconds. The seconds felt like a lifetime.

When the car stopped and my sister and I looked at each other and our boys, the adrenaline was flowing wild and we cried and cried. My son looked at us and said "that was fun, let's do it again"! Then we laughed and laughed.

That was God's hand on our car. God lifted and carefully placed our car out of harm's way. It was at that very moment the true importance of life shone directly at us like a beacon from Heaven. It was as if God literally spoke to us about what was critical in life. The message I took from that unreal event was that when you feel the most helpless, at the worst time in your life, give yourself to God and He will direct your path. It is the message from the "Footprints in the Sand" prayer:

One night a man had a dream. He dreamed He was walking along the beach with the LORD. Across the sky flashed scenes from His life. For each scene He noticed two sets of footprints in the sand. One belonging to Him and the other to the LORD.

When the last scene of His life flashed before Him, he looked back at the footprints in the sand. He noticed that many times along the path of His life there was only one set of footprints. He also noticed that it happened at the very lowest and saddest times of His life.

This really bothered Him and He questioned the LORD about it. LORD you said that once I decided to follow you, you'd walk with me all the way. But I have noticed that during the most troublesome times in my life there is only one set of footprints. I don't understand why when I needed you most you would leave me.

The LORD replied, my precious, precious child, I Love you and I would never leave you! During your times of trial and suffering when you see only one set of footprints, it was then that I carried you. Carolyn Carty, 1963

Self-Respect

· ·

L oving yourself is truly the key to Living Sexy. When you show yourself love and forgive yourself when you fall short, you exhibit a particular peace that you cannot achieve without it.

I want to leave you with a comforting feeling about you. Remember there is no other YOU in the world. Believe in yourself, show love to others, be an example so that someone feeling low may look to you for encouragement or guidance.

Life is short but we have a lifetime to live it day by day. We cannot predict when our time will end. We do have control over how we live our lives every day. Make a choice to spread happiness and avoid those things that make you sad. I am a believer in keeping up with current events but I do NOT watch the news. It feels as if the Media tries to show only the bad people in the world. Many would disagree with me but making this choice affords me the ability to focus and channel my energy to smile and think positively about all the beautiful things and people there are in the world. I choose to believe there are good people everywhere and I look for them every day.

Self-respect and love for others are good ways to manifest your sexy!

You Might Have a Bad Hair Day

....

You might have a bad hair day from time to time. I am so thankful for all the compliments I receive for my hair. While I am very blessed with good genes, I still have a bad hair day from time to time. We all do! What about a bad hair day being a metaphor for when things are just not going right? If someone pulls out in front of you or really makes you mad, you might at first feel anger but then laugh. When you start to laugh about these minor nuisances and really reflect on being happy instead of angry or sad, you feel great. It shows through you. Smiling, laughing and being positive make you sexy.

What if an illness causes temporary or permanent hair loss? That in itself would be life altering. But, wouldn't it be incredible to take this negative scenario and create your own sexy which really can be possible at any time and any stage of your life? How sexy would it be to have a different style or color wig to wear for different occasions and create an individual style that makes a statement about your fabulosity? There are really gorgeous wigs available today and some are so funky and cute that they can reflect your inner beauty. Losing your hair is in itself a victory badge against the disease trying to take your life. When you lose your hair, you could be winning the battle against the disease. So why not adorn yourself with a crown and shine your victory everywhere you go.

Loving yourself at all stages of your life, even scary times, is tantamount to living sexy.

What is My Assignment?

· · · · · · · · · · · · · · · · · · · ·

I enjoy reading and I especially enjoy reading meditational, spiritual and encouraging publications that really help to keep me focused on remembering the important things in life. When I wake up every morning, the first thing I do is look out the window and thank God for the new day, for being alive, for my family and friends and for the astounding beauty each morning brings. I watch the sunrise every day but there are those days when it is cloudy or rainy and I thank God for those days too. Just remember the rain allows us to enjoy the green grass and beautiful flowers. And as Kenny Chesney sings, there definitely is "Something Sexy Bout the Rain".

After my waking up routine, I prepare myself for my reading time. I make a cup of coffee or tea, turn on some soothing music and begin my daily journey. I have found a new publication called "The 40 Day Soul Fast, Your Journey to Authentic Living" by Cindy Trimm and it is a beautiful writing with uplifting concepts that keep me focused and thinking about blessings. In my reading today, the subject was "Asking". The book reiterates through scripture from the Bible that God wants us to ask Him for what we need. I started to think that my life evolved into an incredible journey from the exact moment I stopped living my life based on my own direction and gave it to God fully to give me HIS direction. In today's reading the topic was "What is my assignment"? This made me think back to my younger not so sexy years...

I always remember wondering what my talent was, what was my purpose? That may sound odd but even as a young person, pre-teen, I wondered this frequently. Many of my friends were athletic, very sporty, very coordinated, but I did not participate in any type of organized sports. I didn't enjoy them because I was really, really bad at sports! But thinking back, the things I enjoyed and were good at doing were sailing, swimming, dancing, entertaining and talking. Looking at the line up, it becomes clear my likes were more individually driven instead of group driven. My parents would encourage both my sister and me to express ourselves freely by doing an entertainment production for friends if we wanted to. We would dance and lip sync to at the time "You're the One that I Want" from the movie Grease and because I was the big sister I would choose when I wanted to sing Danny's or Sandy's part. My sister and I will laugh about this even now because I always picked the better parts. She was always so cute and supportive! Another game we used to play was pertaining to small business. I remember my sister and me playing around the ages of 10 and 8 in our room where we made price tags on all the clothes in the closet and one of us would be the store employee and the other would be the customer. Thinking back, that was pretty innovative and it was so much fun.

So wondering what my talent was and feeling like I didn't really have direction was very misleading to me as a young girl. But wow, knowing who I am today and knowing what I bring to the table to all the people with whom I come into contact on a daily basis really confirms what my talent truly is. I can honestly say that my assignment is clear. I started writing *Living Sexy* as a sort of how to book but it is in fact evolving into something more; this is the culmination of my talent – and that is, sharing and communicating what I know that will help make others find the reasons to see why they should feel good and blessed and happy.

I truly believe we are brought together for a divine purpose. I don't know what that is, except that we are here to make a difference in someone else's experience. Maybe certain people are brought to us for our benefit or for even their benefit.

By Living Sexy we can and should help others find and live their sexy too!

The Balance

·······················

I am a Libra. If you are familiar with the signs of the horoscope, this one is represented by the scales, always keeping steady. While I am not a horoscope follower by any means, I do believe that I have the characteristics of this balanced demeanor on a daily basis.

Part of being balanced in your life is the dance we do daily to keep our personal lives fulfilled while maintaining our professional lives in a productive fashion that doesn't completely take over our world. I do need to work on this in my daily life. But it is comforting to align ourselves with others who have similar habits and beliefs and who will work together to support our challenges when we need support.

For example, you realize by now I am an extremely positive person who always looks for the best in every situation and every person. But realistically, I am not a robot and I do have real feelings that I sometimes have to manage to keep my attitude working in the right direction. I think the secret of balance is to be aware of our shortcomings and not dwell on them, but really learn about them and try to work out solutions. Try to catch yourself when you see something not so positive creeping into your head and start the deep breathing exercises. Everything we do that is good for our minds and bodies will benefit us immeasurably. Believe that and live that.

I have been getting my brain back in check and am focusing on the foods I eat and the cocktails I drink. As we age, we get a little more lax here and there and due to our bodies changing, it is important to be in control of the calories we take in. Of course, watching the diet is very challenging, especially if you have a very active social lifestyle! I look at it as a balancing project though. Fad diets can't work because the eating is not realistic. Before a person takes on a new diet routine, the first question to ask yourself is "can I continue this after the 'diet' is done, after my goal weight is achieved" – if the answer is no, don't do it! (Of course, always consult with your doctor before trying any new exercises or diets.) The ups and downs of the seesaw diets are so bad for your entire wellbeing, mind and body. If we define the word diet to mean what we eat daily to maintain a healthy balanced lifestyle making good choices most of the time, then I believe we can work to achieve life-long results.

Balance is Living Sexy.

Cheers To Living Your Best Life!

....

Now you have the opportunity to control how you look at life and all its challenges, fears, trials, pain, love and regret. Start every morning by expressing gratitude for life. Ask God, or the Universe or whatever you may believe in what you can do to be a blessing for someone who needs a blessing. When you go to the coffee shop, share your good cheer and wish the clerk a "good morning" and a "wonderful day" and leave with a smile. Let your attitude shine through you like a beacon of light that others will want to emulate.

There are so many ways we can share joy in the world even if just smiling to one person. You don't know what that person may be going through and just your attitude may be uplifting even for a moment. Know that you do make a difference. Believe that you are amazing and fabulous and share your love with everyone you come into contact with.

Life can be magical.

Start living positively.

Find your fabulosity and keep Living Sexy.